Parenting

The Basics of Becoming a Proactive Parent

ProActive Parenting

FaithHome for Parents

Abingdon Press

PARENTING 101
Copyright © 2004 by Abingdon Press

All rights reserved.
No part of this work may be reproduced or transmitted in any form or by any means, electronic or mechanical, including photocopying and recording, or by any information storage or retrieval system, except as may be expressly permitted by the 1976 Copyright Act or in writing from the publisher. Requests for permission should be addressed to Abingdon Press, P.O. Box 801, 201 Eighth Avenue South, Nashville, TN 37202-0801.

Scripture quotations noted NRSV are taken from the *New Revised Standard Version of the Bible*, copyright 1989 by the Division of Christian Education of the National Council of the Churches of Christ in the United States of America. Used by permission.
All rights reserved.

Those noted NIV are from the HOLY BIBLE, NEW INTERNATIONAL VERSION®. Copyright c 1973, 1978, 1984 by International Bible Society. Used by permission of Zondervan Publishing House. All rights reserved.

Those noted NLT are from *The Holy Bible, New Living Translation*, copyright © 1996. Used by permission of Tyndale House Publishers, Inc. Wheaton, Illinios, 60189.
All rights reserved.

Those noted NCV are quoted from *The Holy Bible, New Century Version*, copyright © 1987, 1988, 1991 by Word Publishing, Nashville, Tennessee, 37214. used by permission.

Scripture taken from THE MESSAGE Copyright © Eugene H. Peterson, 1993, 1994, 1995. Used by permission of NavPress Publishing Group.

Parenting on Point: Leading Your Family Along God's Path by James C. Williams. Copyright 2002 by Abingdon Press, Nashville, Tennessee, 37202. Reprinted by permission.

04 05 06 07 08 09 10 11 12 13—10 9 8 7 6 5 4 3 2 1

MANUFACTURED IN THE UNITED STATES OF AMERICA

Contents

Everything You Need to Know Before You Begin This Study 5

Introducing Jim Williams 9

Week 1
Navigating Through Troubled Waters . . . 11

Week 2
Developing a Parenting Plan 19

Week 3
Managing the "Balancing Act" 27

Week 4
Keeping Your Family Strong. 37

Everything You Need to Know Before You Begin This Study

According to Stephen Covey, author of *The Seven Habits of Highly Effective People,* we have a choice: We can live either in a circle of concern or a circle of influence. When we live in a circle of concern, we're always reacting to events and circumstances. We fail to plan or prepare or look ahead. Often we end up "putting out fires" and racing from one crisis to another. When we live in a circle of influence, on the other hand, we're always one step ahead. Planning and preparation are part of our everyday lives. We know our desired goal, and we plan accordingly in order to achieve it. The *ProActive Parenting* series is about choosing to live in a circle of influence—with God in the center. Simply put, it is about learning how to parent with a plan so that you can become the kind of parent that God wants you to be.

Parenting 101 is intended to help you learn the basics of becoming a proactive parent—a parent who keeps your family headed in the direction God wants you to take. This brings us to two concepts that are foundational to this study as well as the entire *ProActive Parenting* series.

Two Key Concepts

1. The North Star Versus the Artificial Star

Jim Williams, parenting expert, author, and video presenter of this series, says that parenting is similar to navigating: You need an unchanging reference point such as the North Star to help keep you on course. In his book *Parenting on Point,* he explains that this North Star is the moral center of the family, or the core beliefs, values, and principles that help your family to stay on the course God wants you to follow. As Christian parents, your North Star will include biblical beliefs and values—such as those found in the Ten Commandments (Deuteronomy 5:6-21), the Golden Rule (Matthew 7:12), the new commandment of Jesus (Matthew 22:37-40), and the love chapter (1 Corinthians 13)—as well as other important principles that support and strengthen the family.

One of your most important parenting responsibilities is to identify and communicate your North Star. In fact, Jim Williams says that you must *clearly articulate* your North Star if you want to keep your children from being pulled "off course" by an even larger, more magnetic star called the artificial star. The artificial star represents the values of popular culture. It is the cultural ethos that encourages your children to. . .

- ◆ Do what feels good (rather than do what's right)
- ◆ Pursue instant gratification (rather than practice delayed gratification)
- ◆ Look out for "number one" (rather than live the Golden Rule)

Regrettably, the artificial star is bigger today than ever before, and it continues to grow at an exponential rate thanks to the entertainment industry. If you want your children to follow your family's North Star, rather than be pulled off course by the huge artificial star, then you must be proactive in identifying and clearly communicating your values to your children.

2. The Family Mission Statement

One of the most effective ways to communicate your family's values is by writing a family mission statement. If you have already written a family mission statement, then you will want to review it and, if necessary, make any revisions. If you have not already written a family mission statement, then you will begin working on one during Week 2 of this study (see the step-by-step guidelines provided on page 26). Jim Williams encourages you to involve your children in the process, explaining, "If you want your children to 'catch' the core family values, which are reflected in the family mission statement, then they need to feel they are involved in the process of creating that statement" (*Parenting on Point,* p. 37). If your children are not yet in elementary school, their participation and understanding naturally will be limited. Still, even young children can participate in writing a simple mission statement based on the Golden Rule (Matthew 7:12) or the new commandment of Jesus (Matthew 22:37-40).

The process of writing a family mission statement will take several weeks. Set a goal for completion and schedule at least two family "sessions" prior to this date when you may work on it together. You might consider having one or more of these family sessions in a weekend getaway at a hotel, campground, or other setting. This will turn what otherwise might be a dreaded exercise into a fun family experience. However you choose to do it, writing a family mission statement will be an incredibly rewarding exercise that will help to build a strong foundation for your family for many years to come.

Now that you have a basic understanding of what *ProActive Parenting* is all about, let's move on to the basics of how each study works.

A Quick Overview

This four-week study has been designed to be easy to use. The material for each week is divided into three sections: Before Class, During Class, and After Class. In the first section you will find brief background material, called Background Basics, which will prepare you for the group session. You will be able to complete each reading in just a few minutes. *Please don't skip this important step.* Some of the material included here will not be covered in class and will give you additional information that will be beneficial both during and after the group session.

The second section walks you through the one-hour group session, which consists primarily of video segments and group discussion. Jim Williams, a dynamic parenting instructor, will be your "guest speaker" each week. To help you "get acquainted" with Jim, be sure to read the compelling story of why he is so passionate about helping you to become a proactive parent (see pages 9-10).

After viewing each of the first two video segments, you will have the opportunity to discuss several questions that will allow you to share your own thoughts and ideas as well as benefit from others' insights and experiences. If your group has no time constraints, you may want to extend this discussion time, lengthening the total time of the group session. There simply is no substitute for the encouragement and support of other parents whose family values and goals are in line with your own. In fact, you may find your group experience to be so valuable that you will want to do another study in this series together, or choose to continue meeting informally as a parenting support group.

Prayer and scripture are two valuable components of every group session as well. The group facilitator may choose to use the opening and closing prayers provided or create original prayers. In either case, the intent is to "cover" the group session in prayer, acknowledging that we are incapable of being the parents God wants us to be without God's grace, strength, and help. Likewise, the Wisdom from the Word provided for each group session is intended not only to provide a biblical foundation for the group session, but also to highlight relevant verses that you may meditate on throughout the week. Take time each day to read and reflect on the Wisdom from the Word for that week, asking God to show you how these truths apply to your own family life. Hebrews 4:12 tells us that "the word of God is living and active" (NRSV). Likewise, we read in Isaiah 55:11, "My word…shall not return to me empty, but it shall accomplish that which I purpose, and succeed in the thing for which I sent it" (NRSV). If you will seek God's guidance through the Holy Scriptures, you can *expect* to receive the direction and wisdom you desire!

The third and final section of each week's material offers Homework exercises and Tools and Tips that will help you with the practical step of application. Don't let the word "homework" scare you! You will not be asked to "turn in" these exercises or share any details with the group. They are intended for your private use and your family's benefit only.

They are not intended, however, to be "optional." Each exercise is designed to help you get the most out of this study that you possibly can. Whether or not this is just another parenting class or a transformational learning experience that will have a lasting, positive impact on you and your family is up to you. So you are strongly encouraged to complete as much of the Homework assignments as you can each week and to use those Tools and Tips that are applicable to your family. If you do, you will be well on your way to becoming a proactive parent—a parent who chooses to live in a circle of influence with God in the center.

Introducing Jim Williams

God brings special people into our lives to instruct and encourage us along life's journey, and often these people help to change our lives in ways we never could have anticipated. Jim Williams is one of those special people for me and for many, many other parents who have had the privilege of taking one of his parenting courses. One thing that makes Jim so special is that he's not just another "parenting expert." He is a disciple of Jesus Christ who has a God-given mission to help families "get back on track"—on the path that God wants them to follow. Jim's story is best told in his own words. So I invite you to get comfortable and "listen" with both your head and your heart as Jim shares why he is so passionate about helping you to become a better parent—a proactive parent who strives to keep God in the center of your family's life.

Sally Sharpe
Series Editor

My life changed forever on November 11, 1995, when a drunk driver killed my nineteen-year-old son, Curt. That night I came to the full realization that God gives everyone the free will to choose. That night a man exercised his free will to choose, and he chose to drink and then drive his truck home while intoxicated. My world was shattered.

At the time, Curt was a sophomore at Birmingham-Southern College, where he was thriving. Meanwhile, back at home, I was having great difficulty enjoying the parenting experience with my sixteen-year-old daughter, Beth. I was frustrated because she did not "embrace my world" as I thought she should, and we fought all the time.

When the call came from the hospital in Birmingham on the night of Curt's accident, my wife, Carol, left immediately, and I waited to locate Beth, who was out on a date. A few hours later, Beth and I rode all the way to Birmingham without even talking. I sat in the front seat with my minister, and Beth sat in the backseat by herself.

Two days after Curt's funeral, God "opened my eyes." I realized for the first time how distant Beth and I had become. I realized that I needed to change as a parent or I was going to lose Beth, too.

Parenting 101 **9**

Approximately six months after Curt's death, I was advised by my employer of twenty-three years that my business unit was being eliminated and I was losing my job. This action gave me the opportunity to reevaluate my life's work. The fact that this loss happened so soon after the loss of Curt helped to "open my ears" and enabled me to listen to God. I felt that God was leading me to make a difference in the lives of children and parents by combining my lifelong passion for outreach with my recent volunteer work for STARS (Students Taking a Right Stand), a nonprofit organization in the public school system whose mission is to help children make healthy lifestyle choices. So, with incredible support from my family and my peers, I worked to develop a series of educational and motivational speeches and classroom presentations for children, followed by a series of parenting classes and workshops for adults. Ever since, I have been working full-time in the classroom, devoting my days to helping children and my evenings to helping parents.

After continued requests from parents for a printed copy of my "teachings," God engineered circumstances making it possible for the book Parenting on Point *to be born. Now this study series,* ProActive Parenting, *makes it possible for me to reach even more parents via video each week, sharing practical insights on how they can keep God in the center of their lives despite the negative influence of popular culture. There's no limit to what God can do—and that includes what God can do for your family through this study.*

I hope that as you view the video segments each week, you will feel as if we have become friends. As I share my life and the insights I have gained through personal and professional experience, study, and various mentors, my hope is that you will take away better skills to meet the many challenges you face as a parent, and that you will be motivated to use these skills in your daily life. If you do, I promise that not only will you enjoy the parenting experience far more than I did, but also, through a commitment to ProActive Parenting and a renewed commitment to your children, you will find it easier to be the parent that God wants you to be.

Jim Williams

Week 1
Navigating Through Troubled Waters

Before Class

Background Basics

Proactive parenting is choosing to live in a circle of influence. Simply put, it is parenting with a plan. *Parenting 101* is designed to give you the "basics" needed for proactive parenting by walking you through the process of creating a parenting plan tailor made for your family. Let's get started!

Every Family Needs a "North Star"

Every navigator knows that a compass is an essential tool. Years ago, navigators would use the North Star to guide their vessels. Their ability to keep the North Star in view determined whether or not they would be successful in reaching their intended destination.

In a way, parenting is a like navigating a ship or a plane: You need a compass, or as Jim Williams calls it, a "North Star," to help keep you on course. In his book *Parenting on Point,* he explains that this North Star is the moral center of the family, or the core beliefs, values, and principles that help your family to stay on the right course—the course God would have you to follow. As Christian parents, your North Star will include biblical beliefs and values—such as those found in the Ten Commandments (Deuteronomy 5:6-21), the Golden Rule (Matthew 7:12), the new commandment of Jesus (Matthew 22:37-40), and the love chapter (1 Corinthians 13)—as well as important principles and practices that support and strengthen the family such as forgiveness, family worship, servanthood, family time and family fun, fairness, and active listening.

It is important to both identify your North Star and communicate it. In fact, Jim Williams says that you must *clearly articulate* your family's North Star if you want to keep your children from being pulled "off course" by popular culture—what he calls the "artificial star."

Today's Greatest Parenting Challenge: The Artificial Star

Just what is the "artificial star"? It is the cultural ethos that encourages our children to ...

- ◆ Do what feels good (rather than do what's right)
- ◆ Pursue instant gratification (rather than practice delayed gratification)
- ◆ Look out for "number one" (rather than live the Golden Rule)

Regrettably, the artificial star is bigger today than ever before, and it continues to grow exponentially thanks to the entertainment industry. In fact, studies indicate that children today are spending an average of six hours with the entertainment industry each day—sitting in front of the computer, playing video games, and watching TV. Besides the fact that the artificial star has a negative influence on children, especially in regards to drugs, sex, and violence, it gives them no opportunity for relationship building. Jim Williams says that "verbalizing and discussing [our] values is crucial if we are to stay focused and stand firm when that huge magnetic artificial star tries to pull our children—and us—off point" (*Parenting on Point*, p. 36).

Unfortunately, many parents today are passive, wrongly assuming they have little or no power over the negative impact of popular culture. In their view, the pull of the artificial star is more than they can combat. The truth is, we—not pop culture or society—control which star will be most powerful in our children's lives. Though we cannot eliminate pop culture from our children's lives, we can take measures to significantly reduce its negative impact as we simultaneously increase the positive impact of our own family value system.

One of the most effective measures we can take to reduce the negative impact of the artificial star is simply to spend more time talking with our children—without distractions such as the TV, computer, radio, cell phones, and other "noise." Only by increasing the time we spend having meaningful conversations with our children will we be able to help them "catch" our values. When that happens, they view them as their own values and, therefore, have the desire to sustain them.

Your Child's Circle of Adults

Many parents give up trying to "fight" the artificial star, allowing it to become the predominant force in their children's lives because they have no support system. Contrary to the independent mindset of our culture, we cannot do it alone. We cannot fight the magnetism of the artificial star without the help of others who share our values. Williams calls this your child's circle of adults. In addition to parents, our children need other positive adult role models in their lives—adults who share our value system and will do their part to reinforce the family's North Star and keep our children on course.

Establishing a circle of adults for our children requires us to be proactive. It is our responsibility as parents to ensure that our children have at least three positive adult role models in their lives at all times. These adults might include grandparents, uncles and aunts, teachers, Sunday school teachers, friends, neighbors, coaches, Scout leaders, and others. This kind of support network benefits not only our children but also ourselves. As Ecclesiastes 4:9-12 reminds us, there is strength and stability in numbers:

> *Two are better than one, because they have a good reward for their toil. For if they fall, one will lift up the other; but woe to one who is alone and falls and does not have another to help. Again, if two lie together, they keep warm; but how can one keep warm alone? And though one might prevail against another, two will withstand one. A threefold cord is not quickly broken. (NRSV)*

When God is the uniting "thread" among us, the cord is stronger yet—stronger than even the magnetic artificial star.

During Class

In Focus

The purpose of this session is to explore the negative impact of popular culture on your family and to consider the importance of being proactive in your parenting by identifying and articulating your family's core beliefs and values.

Wisdom from the Word

Teach your children to choose the right path, and when they are older, they will remain upon it. (Proverbs 22:6 NLT)

Opening Prayer

Dear loving and gracious God, you have given us the responsibility of teaching our children to choose the right path—the path that you want them to follow—and of guiding them along that path. We humbly acknowledge our inability to do this without your help, and we come today seeking your wisdom, guidance, and strength. Open our eyes and our ears so that we may be more aware than ever before of the need to be proactive and intentional in our parenting, and help us to become the parents you would have us to be. Amen.

Video Segment 1

Candid Kids
Running Time: 1:37

Discussion Questions
1. Did you gain any insights from the children's comments?
2. Was there one comment that caught your attention more than others?

Video Segment 2

A Parent's Perspective
Running Time: 15:32 minutes

Group Discussion
1. Read aloud this week's Wisdom from the Word (page 13). How can identifying and communicating the core values or "North Star" of your family help you to keep your children on the "right path"? What potential challenges or obstacles might you face?
2. Identify some of the negative influences of the artificial star (popular culture) on your family. What can you do to decrease these negative influences and increase the positive influences of your family's North Star?
3. What can you do to ensure that each of your children has at least three positive adult roles models in his or her life? What criteria will you use to "select" these individuals?

Video Segment 3

In Summary
Running Time: 0:53 minutes

Closing Prayer

Dear Lord, thank you for this time of learning and fellowship. Thank you for the insights you've given us related to our essential role in keeping our children on the right path. Help us to set aside time this week to talk about what constitutes our own family's North Star and to complete our homework assignments for next time. Amen.

After Class

Homework

1. Discuss the class session. What new insight(s) or understanding(s) did you gain? What do you believe will be of greatest benefit to you/your family?

_____

_____

2. Talk about what constitutes your family's North Star (moral center, family value system). What are the core values, beliefs, and principles that help to keep your family on the right path—God's path? Record these in the space that follows. (You'll need this list as you begin to write a family mission statement in Week 2.)

_____

_____

_____

_____

3. Read the Background Basics for Week 2.

Tools and Tips

The ABC's of ProActive Parenting

A ssess yourself periodically by...
- keeping a "conversation log" beside your bed. Each night before bedtime, record the number of minutes you spent talking with each child that day. How many of these minutes were spent saying something positive?
- monitoring your family life. Rate yourselves daily on how well you model your family values (1 being poor, 5 being strong). What insights do you gain?
- examining the artificial star's "pull" on your family. Briefly jot down any influences that contradict or compromise your family's North Star (core beliefs/values) and your responses to each. What changes, if any, do you need to make?

B egin early talking with your children about sex, drugs, the entertainment world, and violence. Maintain *regular* conversations about these subjects throughout your children's years at home. In addition to talking about the practical aspects of each subject, be sure to talk about the emotional and spiritual aspects as well, discussing each subject in the context of your family's values and beliefs. (You may collect information about the various drugs your children will come in contact with and the dangers associated with them by talking with teachers and guidance counselors in your children's schools and doing your "homework." An excellent resource is the National Clearing House for Alcohol and Drug Information [1-800-729-6686].

C urtail the impact of the entertainment world on your children. (See the list of suggested ideas that follow.)

(Information adapted from *Parenting on Point,* p. 25.)

Ways to Curtail the Impact of the Entertainment World
1. Limit the amount of time your children spend watching TV/videos. Determine a reasonable daily limit and stick to it!
2. Don't use TV/videos as a babysitter; watch together
3. Don't rely on the rating system used by the networks and film/music industries. Screen television shows, movies, music, and videos in advance, if possible, or evaluate the content through reviews on Web sites.
4. Always explain why certain content is inappropriate or unacceptable,

discussing the material in the context of your family's North Star.
5. Don't hesitate to change the channel or leave the theater. Then, use this opportunity to discuss and reinforce your family's values and beliefs.
6. Always set a good example for your children, including your own practices related to alcohol and drugs (including nicotine) and your TV/movie viewing habits.

(Adapted from *Parenting on Point*, p. 30)

Week 2

Developing a Parenting Plan

Before Class

Background Basics

Have you ever heard of a winning sports team that didn't practice before a game, or an exceptional teacher who didn't prepare before a class, or a renowned architect who didn't draft a set of plans before construction began? Of course not! Being effective in any endeavor requires planning and preparation. Parenting is no different. Unfortunately, many parents choose to "shoot from the hip" rather than to be proactive parents, and both they and their children suffer the consequences.

Our Wisdom from the Word last week was Proverbs 22:6, which gives us this instruction: "Teach your children to choose the right path, and when they are older, they will remain upon it" (NLT). As we've seen, the first step is to identify "the right path"—to identify our core beliefs and values, our North Star. Once we have done this, then we are ready to begin constructing a parenting plan that will help us to keep our children on this path, following our North Star. Though Jim Williams admits that having a parenting plan won't keep us from making mistakes and getting off track occasionally, he says that, by keeping us focused on our North Star, a parenting plan will redirect us and get us back on God's path (*Parenting on Point,* pp. 12-13).

Parenting Philosophies and Expectations

So, how do you create your parenting plan? Actually, you've already begun by discussing and listing the important beliefs, values, and priorities of your family—your family's North Star. Many parents also find it helpful to discuss their childhood families, their parents' approaches to parenting, and their own parenting expectations and objectives. The point is to come to agreement about what constitutes "good parenting." Ideally, we should discuss these matters before our children arrive, but it's never too late to begin.

If you will take time to explore your individual philosophies of parenting and your own experiences, both as a child and as a parent, you will gain a better understanding of each other's parenting preferences and identify possible problem areas. Some of the topics you might discuss include the following:

- What kind of atmosphere do you want to have in your home?
- What kind of family life do you want to have? (Describe a typical day.)
- What kind of parent do you want to be? (Write a description.)
- What kind of behavior do you want family members to demonstrate?
- What goals will you have for your children at various stages of their lives?
- What are your fondest childhood memories, and how can you help your children have similar experiences?
- What are the painful experiences you had with your parents that you want to avoid with your children?
- What kinds of rules and responsibilities do you believe children need?
- What were your parents' mode(s) of discipline, and to what extent do you plan to use the same techniques?
- What kind of changes do you need to make in your family to have more fun together?

The Family Mission Statement

In addition to having conversations about your parenting philosophies and expectations, writing a family mission statement is an essential component of an effective parenting plan. Jim Williams writes in *Parenting on Point*, "Children need a clear sense of direction, and they need that direction to be articulated. A family mission statement does both" (pp. 36-37). He strongly encourages parents to involve the children in writing the family mission statement, admitting that the participation and understanding of children who are not yet in elementary school naturally will be limited. Still, even young children can participate in writing a simple mission statement based on the Golden Rule (Matthew 7:12) or the new commandment of Jesus (Matthew 22:37-40). He explains, "If you want your children to 'catch' the core family values, which are reflected in the family mission statement, then they need to feel they are involved in the process of creating that statement" (*Parenting on Point,* p. 37).

Another piece of advice is to give it ample time. According to Williams, a good family mission statement requires at least two drafts and more than one family session. You might consider having one or more of these family sessions in a weekend getaway at a hotel, campground, or other setting. This will turn what otherwise might be a dreaded exercise into a fun family experience.

Finally, as the Nike saying goes, "Just do it!" Many parents tell their children that they're going to write a family mission statement and then never do it. Others write a first draft and never see it through to completion. As Williams says, "Your lack of commitment will speak volumes" (*Parenting on Point,* p. 37).

You will explore the family mission statement in more detail in the video for this session. For step-by-step instructions for the process of writing your own family mission statement, see Tools and Tips on page 26.

Core Commitments / Goals and Objectives

Another key component of an effective parenting plan is a list of core commitments you must make in order to live out your family mission statement. You might think of this as your "action plan." Jim Williams explains: "As I learned in the business world, a mission statement alone isn't enough. Just as every business unit must develop an annual business plan to support its mission statement, so also every family must develop an annual action plan to support their mission statement" (*Parenting on Point,* p. 50). He encourages families to make commitments to things such as a moral framework (e.g., the Ten Commandments, the Golden Rule, Jesus' New Commandment, etc.), church involvement, family time, a healthy lifestyle, safety, education, and a family budget (*Parenting on Point,* pp. 50-52). You might want to use this list as a starting point and adapt it or add to it as necessary to support your own family's mission statement.

Once you have identified the core commitments your family needs to make in order to implement your mission statement, write them in the format of goals or objectives. For example, if a core commitment of your family is church, you might write several objectives, such as "We will attend church and Sunday school regularly"; "Every family member will be involved in at least one church activity/group in addition to Sunday school"; "We will participate as a family in at least one service/outreach project a year"; and so forth. Once you have done this for each core commitment, you will have a list of family goals and objectives for the year. Of course, you'll want to review and update this list of objectives, as well as your core commitments and family mission statement, each year.

Unique to You

As you begin creating your own parenting plan, remember that both the process and the outcome will be unique to you. There's no right or wrong way to go about it. The important thing is that you find a way to sort through all the experiences and expectations you bring and form your own clearly communicated set of shared values and objectives—expressed through your family mission statement and core commitments. Keep in mind that every family is different, and, therefore, no two family mission statements or lists of core commitments/objectives will be identical.

Remember, also, that friends and extended family members sometimes can be critical instead of supportive when you reflect a difference in beliefs, values, priorities, or parenting styles from their own. So it is important during the process of creating your own parenting plan that you guard against any discouragement or conflict caused by outside influences. Focus on the direction God would have you to lead your family, and you will be well on your way to creating a strong family.

During Class

In Focus

The purpose of this session is to prepare you to discuss what constitutes "good parenting" and to develop your own parenting plan, drawing upon biblical guidelines, your own experiences, and credible parenting authorities.

Wisdom from the Word

But those who plan what is good find love and faithfulness. (Proverbs 14:22b NIV)

Opening Prayer

Dear God, we come here today acknowledging our need to keep you in the center of our families and seeking your help and guidance for the challenging task of parenting. Give us the wisdom and understanding we need to be proactive parents, leading our children along the right path. Amen.

Core values & commitments

Video Segment 1

Candid Kids
Running Time: 1:46 minutes

Discussion Questions
1. Did you gain any insights from the children's comments?
2. Was there one comment that caught your attention more than others?

Video Segment 2

A Parent's Perspective
Running Time: 13:00 minutes

Group Discussion
1. Read aloud this week's Wisdom from the Word (page 22). How can writing a family mission statement help you to "plan what is good" and "find love and faithfulness" in your family?
2. In this week's video, Jim Williams suggests four core values or commitments that could be included in a family mission statement: unconditional love, respect, church participation, and mutual encouragement and support. What additional "core values" would you want to include in your family mission statement?
3. What does it mean for you to love your children *unconditionally*? What changes do you need to make, and what help do you need?

Video Segment 3

In Summary
Running Time: 0:56 minutes

Closing Prayer
Lord, thank you for this time of learning and fellowship. Thank you for the insights you've given us related to the planning necessary for effective parenting. Help us to set aside time this week to begin developing our own parenting plan as we complete our homework assignments for next time. Amen.

After Class

Homework

1. Discuss the class session. What new insight(s) or understanding(s) did you gain? What do you believe will be of greatest benefit to you/your family?

   _____
   _____
   _____

2. Take turns sharing your thoughts about what constitutes "good parenting," drawing upon biblical guidelines, your own experiences, and insights you've gained from credible parenting authorities. Explain why you believe each of these attributes or practices is important. Listen attentively to each other, asking questions for clarification while holding all other comments until your spouse has finished speaking. Identify any areas of disagreement and search to find out what the Bible has to say, as well as other Christian resources. Consider talking with a pastor or Christian counselor, if necessary, in order to work through any potentially divisive issues. (Note: Single parents can have this discussion with a mentor or pastor or other highly respected individual, seeking feedback rather than agreement.)

3. Good parenting is…_____
   _____
   _____
   _____
   _____
   _____
   _____

4. Begin working on a family mission statement, following the instructions on page 26. Remember that it will require several weeks to complete your family mission statement. Try to complete step #1 this week, and schedule times on your calendar for completing the remaining steps. If possible, make plans for a fun family getaway where you can have a brainstorming session, write a first draft, and enjoy time together. Set a target completion date for your finished statement

   These things are central to keeping our family headed in the right direction:

   _____

   _____

   _____

   _____

   _____

   _____

5. Read the Background Basics for Week 3.

Tools and Tips

Other Tips for Creating a Parenting Plan
1. Draft a one- to two- paragraph description of the kind of parent you would like to be. Remember to keep it simple. Refer to this description periodically to see "how you're doing."
2. Discuss potentially difficult parenting scenarios and how you would respond in each situation. Consider writing an "If…then…" statement for each one. For example, "If our child were to get a failing grade on a report card, we would…." (Note: Single parents can have this discussion with a family member or other respected individual.)
3. Talk with an older couple you respect and admire whose children are grown. Encourage them to tell stories of their successes and failures. Ask them to tell you what they would do differently and what they would do the same if they could start their family again.

How to Write a Family Mission Statement
1. Identify those things that are central to your ability to keep your family headed in the right direction. This includes, but is not limited to, your core values and beliefs.
2. As a family, have a brainstorming session around these topics. Allow family members to add ideas of their own without critique. "No idea is a bad idea."
3. Work together to identify core ideas and common threads.
4. Put the core ideas and common threads into salient points. This is your first draft.
5. Post your first draft, or give each family member a copy, and "let it simmer" for a while.
6. Review your mission statement together as a family.
7. Make revisions and finalize it.
8. Print it, frame it, and hang it.

Next steps...
1. Identify core commitments that will enable you to live out your mission statement (e.g., a commitment to a moral framework, church involvement, family time, a healthy lifestyle, a family budget, etc.).
2. Write a list of yearly family goals and objectives based on your core commitments; print them and post them.

(Adapted from *Parenting on Point,* pp. 48-49)

Week 3
Managing the "Balancing Act"

Before Class

Background Basics

Are you a good juggler? As a parent, you'd better be! Just think about it: You have many "balls" to juggle—children, children's activities, a spouse (if married) and his or her activities, work, family obligations and responsibilities, friends, personal interests, and more. Considering that the strength of your family depends directly upon your physical and mental well being, it's essential that you maintain a high level of wellness. But how is that possible when you have more balls than you can juggle successfully? The key lies in letting your family's North Star be the determining factor when making decisions about how you and your family will spend your time.

When we choose to be proactive parents and live in a circle of influence rather than a circle of concern, we're always one step ahead. Planning, preparation, and disciplined follow-through are part of our everyday lives. Obviously, this requires time management skills. Ironically, many parents practice time management skills at work yet fail to practice the same principles in their family life. Those parents who do practice time management principles in their families often fail to connect those principles with the family's core beliefs and values. Only when we weave the two together—time management and the family's North Star—is it possible to manage the balancing act. This week we will consider how you can do just that.

Setting Priorities

Most time management courses use what's called the ABC approach. The As on our "to do" list are those things that must be addressed immediately. The Bs are those things that are important but can wait a while. The Cs are those things that should be done only after all of the As and Bs have been addressed. The key to successfully implementing this approach in family life is to make sure that all As and Bs on your family calendar and your "to do" list are in line with your family's North Star and core commitments. It is not necessary, however, for Cs to support your North Star or core commitments—although they certainly should not contradict them. As psychologist and author Bobbie Reed explains, As and Bs should be tasks that help you focus on your God-given priorities and achieve related goals. She writes,

> For example, teaching our children how to live according to God's standards is a biblical priority (Deuteronomy 6:7). It follows then, that spending time with each child and providing a strong spiritual influence by reading and discussing Bible stories, praying together, and teaching our children positive biblical values are critical parenting tasks that help us focus on this priority and achieve specific goals we might set related to this priority. Other tasks also may be important, but all tasks are not equally important. Prayerfully setting your priorities, then, is the first step toward… discerning which tasks are more important" ("Your Family and Time Management," FaithHome for Parents, Abingdon Press, 2000, pp. 2-3).

When you follow this approach to setting priorities, you are putting faith and family first.

Setting Limits

Putting faith and family first, however, does not always mean putting the children first. Consider the infamous "soccer mom." Her children do not always play soccer. Sometimes it's baseball or basketball or gymnastics or dance or piano. Anyway, she's the mom who never says no to anything and has more tasks to complete than time allowed. The results are obvious. Everyone in the family becomes frustrated and unhappy. By the way, dads are not exempt from this pitfall. Many dads try to excel at work and be "Super Dad" by attending every practice and game or coaching multiple teams. The point is, many parents are stressed out because they assume that in order to be good parents, they must give every activity related to their children an A priority. They wind up having too many As on their plate!

Every activity, event, task, and commitment cannot be an A. There have to be some Bs and Cs, which means that you must carefully evaluate each activity or item in light of your North Star and core commitments. In order to uphold your family's commitment to church involvement, for example, you may have to say no to other worthwhile activities from time to time. At one time or another, you may need to turn down a work opportunity or make a job change in order to increase your time with your family. (Stephen Covey suggests in *The Seven Habits of Highly Effective Families* that, ideally, two-parent families have no more than 1.5 jobs. Jim Williams says more about this in the video.) Sometimes you may need to make rest and relaxation an A while making another activity a B or C—especially on Sunday, which has become just another day of stress for many families. Perhaps you may even need to eliminate some activities from your schedule altogether—at least for the time being. Managing the "balancing act" requires learning when to say "no." If saying "no" is difficult for you, it's especially important for you to keep your focus on your priorities by setting limits *in advance*.

As parents begin evaluating priorities and setting limits, they often wonder how many activities outside school a child should be allowed to participate in at one time. According to Jim Williams, the answer is generally one. He clarifies this by saying that the number and nature of activities should not cause any undue stress in the family. Of course, each of us has a different tolerance for stress, and so only you can determine what is manageable for you and your family. Likewise, only you can determine if the chosen activities are in line with your family's North Star.

Many parents also wonder how many of their children's activities they should regularly attend. According to Jim Williams, the underlying question here is really, *How much is enough to show my child that I love him or her?* He says there are so many ways and opportunities to make your child feel loved, that going to *every* practice, game, or other repetitive event is unnecessary. Of course, special or less frequent events, such as recitals and play performances, are a different matter and always should be attended to support and encourage your child's talents and abilities.

Delegating and Sharing Tasks

As you set priorities and limits, determining which activities and tasks are more important than others, remember that you don't have to do it all. Bobbie Reed says that "most of us learn early on in the parenting game that many tasks and responsibilities can be delegated or shared. For example, older children can read to younger siblings, children of all ages can help with chores, carpools can be organized with friends and neighbors, and so forth" ("Your Family and Time Management," p. 3). Why, then, do many parents opt not to delegate tasks or enlist the help of others? There are two primary reasons: 1) They don't want to take the time to give instructions to someone else, and 2) They want to retain control. Though there are some exceptions to the rule, generally it requires less time to make the necessary arrangements than it will take to do a given task yourself. Likewise, the number of tasks requiring your particular expertise is few in comparison to the number that can be effectively delegated or shared with others. Most often, delegating and sharing tasks is a winning proposition for both you and your family.

Taking Time to Relax

We've said that the strength of your family depends directly upon your physical and mental well being, which means that rest and relaxation should be a regular, planned part of your family's routine. Ironically, for many families today, rest and relaxation have become stressful activities in and of themselves. This is especially true of the family vacation. Making arrangements, packing, and traveling are stressful enough without the added stress of conflicts about how to spend your time and money. Often the vacation is almost over before everyone is able to actually "wind down" and relax. Jim Williams recommends that, if possible, you stretch your next vacation beyond one week, even if for only a few days. Another idea he suggests is to have one parent—or another adult traveling with you—be the "vacation coordinator." Each person writes on a piece of paper the number one activity he or she wants to do. The only ground rules are that the cost of the activity cannot exceed a predetermined amount, and the activity cannot contradict the family's North Star. The coordinator's job is to ensure that all number one activities are accomplished before the next to last day of vacation. (*Parenting on Point,* p. 163)

In addition to a family vacation, it's helpful to plan regular times of rest and relaxation for the entire family, as well as time for yourself and time with your spouse (if married). These times of rest and relaxation will not only help you to reduce your stress but also to nurture your relationships. In fact, when you follow each of the basic guidelines we've considered—identifying what is important (setting priorities), learning when to say "no" (setting limits), being able to let go when appropriate (delegating and sharing tasks), and taking time to relax, you focus your attention on God's priorities, freeing you from unnecessary and harmful stress and allowing you to give your time and energy to loving one another.

During Class

In Focus
The purpose of this session is to help you focus on your God-given priorities by making your North Star the determining factor when choosing how you and your family will spend your time.

Wisdom from the Word
Figure out what will please Christ, and then do it. Don't waste your time on useless work, mere busywork, the barren pursuits of darkness.... So watch your step. Use your head. Make the most of every chance you get.... Don't live carelessly, unthinkingly. Make sure you understand what the Master wants. (Ephesians 5: 10-17 The Message)

Opening Prayer
Sovereign God, you are the master of all time and the priority of life, yet how often our individual lives fail to reflect this reality. We've allowed ourselves to become overscheduled and overstressed, shifting our focus from you and your priorities to so many useless and unimportant things. Give us insight today, Lord, into the changes we need to make in how we spend our time. Help us to slow down and refocus our attention on your and your plans for our lives. Amen.

Video Segment 1

Candid Kids
Running Time: 1:23 minutes

Discussion Questions
1. Did you gain any insights from the children's comments?
2. Was there one comment that caught your attention more than others?

Video Segment 2

A Parent's Perspective
Running Time: 13:02 minutes

Group Discussion
1. What things make it difficult for you to successfully "juggle" your family's busy schedule? Read aloud this week's Wisdom from the Word.

Parenting 101

How can this verse help you in making choices and maintaining balance?
2. How might the ABC approach to prioritizing be useful to your family?
3. Do you agree or disagree with the suggested "ideal" of 1-1.5 jobs for the two-parent family? Why?

Video Segment 3:

In Summary
Running Time: 0:52 minutes

Closing Prayer
Dear Lord, thank you for this time of learning and fellowship. Thank you for the insights you've given us related to setting priorities and managing our time. Help us to begin putting these insights into practice this week as we set aside time to talk about needed changes and to complete our homework assignments for next time. Amen.

After Class

Homework

1. Discuss the class session. What new insight(s) or understanding(s) did you gain? What do you believe will be of greatest benefit to you/your family?

_____

_____

2. Involve the family in creating a "pie chart" on a separate piece of paper to reflect how your family spends your time in an average week. Does your chart support the core values and priorities communicated in your family mission statement and core commitments? As part of this discussion, consider the nature and number of your children's activities in light of your family's North Star. What changes in your family's weekly activities and schedule need to be made? Write a plan of action below, indicating when you will begin implementing each change.

Change / Action	Date to Begin
_____	_____
_____	_____
_____	_____
_____	_____
_____	_____

3. Write a list of tasks and activities for the coming week. Now mark each item according to its ABC priority:

   A (in line with North Star and must be addressed immediately)
   B (in line with North Star but can wait)
   C (not necessarily in line with North Star and should wait until As and Bs have been addressed)

Date / Task	Priority
_____	_____
_____	_____
_____	_____
_____	_____
_____	_____
_____	_____
_____	_____

As you review each item on your list, be sure to ask yourself this question: Can this task/responsibility be reduced, delayed, deleted, delegated, or shared with others? Make this process a weekly habit before the start of each new week.

4. Read the Background Basics for Week 4.

Tools and Tips

10 "Do's" of Time Management

1. Compare how your family spends time now with how you would like your family to spend time in the future.
2. Prayerfully determine your family priorities and goals (based on your North Star and core commitments); then determine which tasks/activities can be eliminated or tabled (Cs), which can be reduced or postponed (Bs), and which must be continued (As). Continually seek God's guidance as you develop, follow, and refine a workable family schedule (see James 1:5).
3. Each weekend, have a family meeting to review the events, activities, and tasks of the coming week.
4. Each evening, plan the details for the next day.
5. Learn to handle interruptions appropriately.
6. Avoid time wasters such as talking too long on the telephone, watching television, backtracking, re-doing something the children have done "incorrectly," lecturing the children (as opposed to talking effectively), reading junk mail, worrying, complaining, wishing things were different, and listening poorly.
7. Minimize daily arguments or unnecessary discussions with a little creativity, such as setting out clothing the night before; using a kitchen timer to signal when to get out of the bathtub, do homework, go to bed, share a toy, etc.; developing an equitable plan for who takes a bath first on which days of the week, who rides in the front seat of the car this time, who does which chores, who chooses the evening television program, and so forth.
8. Use unexpected free time wisely.
9. Reschedule tasks/events that did not get accomplished but are important.
10. Listen once; listen well. Learn to ask good questions, and do your best to ensure that you don't get misinformation.

(Adapted from "Your Family and Time Management," Bobbie Reed, FaithHome for Parents, Abingdon Press, 2000, pp. 3-7)

5 "Don'ts" of Time Management
1. Don't trust your memory. (Write things down.)
2. Don't try to go overboard and plan activities so close together that the slightest variance upsets the schedule for the rest of the day.
3. Don't allow feelings or moods—your own or those of family members—to determine whether or not the schedule is followed.
4. Don't view your schedule in a negative light. (Since each item in your plan is a mini-goal, your schedule becomes a list of achievements as you complete and cross off each item.)
5. Don't be too hard on yourself when you encounter initial setbacks in your schedule. (Remember that time management requires juggling many variables and is not learned overnight.)

Everyday Timesavers

Make the commute to and from work productive by...
- listening to motivational tapes, music, books on tape
- dictating memos, letters, reports
- thinking through problems/issues
- enjoying the solitude
- sleeping, reading, or writing (if not driving)

Turn off the TV during family mealtime and...
- spend time enjoying one another's company
- learn about interesting and important topics
- help children learn to say mealtime prayers
- make family decisions
- catch up on what's happening this week; discuss the family calendar
- converse about one another's interests
- instill morals and values; discuss a Bible verse
- teach fundamental social skills

Break free from the tyranny of the telephone by...
- having and sticking to an agenda
- specifying at the beginning of a call the amount of time you have to talk
- grouping your calls at a convenient time (when making calls)
- using the answering machine (to avoid phone tag and to allow you to schedule call-backs at a convenient time)

Turn "dead" waiting time into productive time by...
- reading, studying, praying, listening to music
- writing/dictating letters, notes, memos, lists, plans
- knitting or doing other handiwork
- making telephone calls from a cell phone or pay phone
- relaxing (relaxing or resting does not necessarily = wasting time!)

"Redeem" time spent on routine chores by...
- doing chores alongside your children and/or spouse to spend time together (reward yourselves with a fun activity or treat afterward)
- doing all chores on Saturday morning so that weekday evenings are free
- doing chores while listening to music, motivational tapes, books on tape, etc.
- assigning specific chores to individual family members
- playing "beat the clock" (set a timer and try to complete chores before the timer goes off)
- thinking through issues or praying while you work (see 1 Thessalonians 5:17)

Week 4
Keeping Your Family Strong

Before Class

Background Basics

Just as a healthy body has an immune system, a healthy family has an "immune system" of its own. Parenting experts affirm that a family can create protective factors that act as a shield against dangers or risks. This week we will look at three of these protective factors:

- Nurturing the marriage relationship
- Establishing a family identity through family traditions and a "signature" family activity
- Sharpening your parenting skills

As a proactive parent, it is your responsibility to do all you can to ensure that these protective factors are working to keep your family strong.

Keeping Your Marriage Strong

One of the most important ways to keep your family strong is to keep your marriage strong, and there's no better way to do this than to learn how to communicate your love for your spouse. In their book *The Five Love Languages,* Gary Chapman and Bill Campbell explain that people have different communication styles and techniques— what they call "love languages." They identify three primary love languages:

Parenting 101 **37**

- ◆ Physical touch (e.g., hugging, kissing, holding hands, backrubs, sexual intimacy in marriage)
- ◆ Words of affirmation/praise (e.g., words of affection, endearment, praise, encouragement, loving tone of voice)
- ◆ Quality time (e.g., undivided attention when communicating, one-on-one time, both with and without verbal communication)

They also identify two secondary love languages, which they say should be used only to strengthen the primary languages—not to replace them:

- ◆ Gifts (e.g., small tokens of affection; flowers, food, or other "treats" that say "You're special"; special surprise purchases; anticipated or desired items)
- ◆ Acts of service (e.g., providing help, handling an undesirable or repetitive task or chore, doing something you know will be appreciated)

When you know which primary language best fits your partner, it is much easier to do a better job of communicating love and support.

Another obvious and yet often neglected way to keep your marriage strong is to spend time alone together on a regular basis. Robert and Jeanette Lauer, marriage and family experts and authors of numerous books, point out that "marriage time," or the time you spend together as a couple, is not the same as family time or friend time. They write:

> Children often swallow up marriage time. Marriage, as a distinct and separate relationship, can even lose its identity "after kids."
> …Work also interferes with marriage time. Too many hours spent on the job—whether at the office or at home—may leave too little time together. Even if you don't work overtime but typically allow work to occupy your thoughts when you are together, your relationship will falter. There are times, of course, when work demands will require extra attention and take away from your time together. But this should be the exception rather than the rule. ("Keeping Marriage Alive," FaithHome for Parents, Abingdon Press, 2001, pp. 2-3)

It's surprising how many couples allow the busyness and fatigue of work and family to keep them from having even a few minutes of uninterrupted "alone time" together on a daily basis. Despite your busy schedules, make it a priority to find a few minutes each day when you can "connect" and express your love for each other. On some days, this may have to take place over the phone lines, especially if one spouse is out of town. Other days, your only available time might be first thing in the morning or a few minutes before closing your eyes at night, but those few minutes can make a huge difference in your relationship.

Marriage experts also encourage parents to set aside one night each week for "just the two of you." If your children are young, make arrangements for a babysitter—preferably a grandparent or other relative, if possible, or a trusted adult friend. If this is not possible, then have a "date" at home after the children are in bed! Prepare a special dinner together, watch a movie, listen to music, or simply enjoy talking and being together. If a weekly date night is unrealistic, then plan one for every other week or, at the very least, once a month.

Likewise, an occasional overnight or weekend getaway is a great way to reconnect and "rekindle the flame." If finances are a concern, consider options such as staying in a reasonably priced local hotel, "trading houses" with relatives or friends, or going to a nearby state park. If grandparents are available to keep the children, it becomes a win-win-win situation! The children enjoy their grandparents; the grandparents enjoy their grandchildren; and you enjoy each other.

Finally, a shared faith is another factor in a strong marriage. As Robert and Jeanette Lauer explain, "In marriage, God gives you a unique opportunity to encourage and build up each other spiritually." They offer these suggestions for growing spiritually as a couple:

- Worship and pray together.
- Talk about how to live out your faith in your daily life and how you can help and support each other.
- Include conversations about spiritual matters as part of your couple-time discussions.
- Share your spiritual journeys, including your individual beliefs and spiritual concerns.
- Be a safe haven for each other, so that you are free to express the struggles, uncertainties, hopes, and joys of your faith.

(From "Keeping Marriage Alive," p. 7)

Remember that in all of these ways—expressing your love for each other, spending time together, and sharing your faith—your goal is to create a strong marriage. And a strong marriage translates to a loving home—one of the best gifts you can give your children.

Establishing a Family Identity

Another way to keep both your marriage and your family strong is to work on establishing a family identity, and the key to building a family identity is shared experiences. One of the most effective ways to create shared experiences is to find a "signature" family activity—an activity that the entire family does together *willingly*. For some families, this might be boating, camping, biking, hiking, or ice skating. Other families might choose to have a regular "family night" when they eat pizza and watch a video or play games together. You might let the children take turns picking the family activity. The thing to remember is that every family member has to participate. If one activity isn't a "hit," then try another until you find something everyone will enjoy.

Family traditions are another great way to create memorable shared experiences. Holidays such as Thanksgiving, Christmas, New Year's Eve/Day, Valentines, and Easter are wonderful opportunities for establishing family traditions, as well as special days such as birthdays, anniversaries, the first and last days of school, awards days, and other days of recognition or celebration. In addition to carrying on traditions from your childhood families, be sure to create a few new family traditions that are exclusively yours. These kinds of shared family activities and traditions will build family relationships while giving your children a strong sense of belonging, security, and self-confidence

Sharpening Your Parenting Skills

A third way to keep your family strong is to be intentional about sharpening your parenting skills. Most parents admit that they have less knowledge about childhood behavior and effective parenting skills than they would like to have. Most parents also admit they would like to become better parents. Yet many parents let the busyness of life keep them from pursuing the skills and knowledge they desire.

Jim Williams recommends that both parents take a parenting course *together*—not only in the early days of parenting, but also periodically through the years. After all, as your children grow and change, you will need to recall or "refresh" what you've already learned as well as to gain pertinent information and skills for handling new situations and challenges. When a parenting course is not available or feasible, Williams suggests that you attend a two-day parenting retreat. These kinds of learning opportunities enable you to become a united "parenting team"—rather than two individuals with different objectives and approaches. They also give you understanding regarding problem areas, as well as specific tools for addressing these areas.

In addition to taking classes, you can sharpen your parenting skills by reading books on parenting and child development, as well as by sharing notes with other parents. Some parents find it beneficial to join a parent support group—or form one of their own. Many churches have Sunday school classes especially for parents of children in particular age groups. Generally, there are more opportunities available than parents realize. The question, then, is which ones are right for you?

Set a yearly goal for your "continuing parenting education," and work toward it. You and your entire family will be glad you did!

During Class

In Focus

The purpose of this session is to identify and explore three protective factors that can help to keep your family strong: 1) Nurturing the marriage relationship, 2) Establishing a family identity, and 3) Sharpening your parenting skills.

Wisdom from the Word

It takes wisdom to have a good family; and it takes understanding to make it strong. It takes knowledge to fill a home with rare and beautiful treasures. (Proverbs 24:3-4 NCV)

Opening Prayer

Lord God, we know that your desire is for us to have strong families, and we acknowledge that you are the Source of our strength. Give us understanding, wisdom, and insight as we explore some of the practical ways we can strengthen our families, and give us the desire and discipline to begin applying what we learn this week. Amen.

Video Segment 1

Candid Kids
Running Time: 1:51

Discussion Questions
1. Did you gain any insights from the children's comments?
2. Was there one comment that caught your attention more than others?

Video Segment 2

A Parent's Perspective
Running Time: 11:37 minutes

Group Discussion
1. Read aloud this week's Wisdom from the Word. How, specifically, can wisdom and knowledge help you to keep your family strong?
2. What are some simple ways you can nurture your marriage on a regular basis?
3. What are the benefits of having a "signature" family activity? What is, or what could be, a "signature" activity for your family?
4. What are some of the obstacles to having a regular "family time" or "family night" each week? What can you do to overcome these obstacles?

Video Segment 3:

In Summary
Running Time: 0:41 minutes

Closing Prayer
Dear Lord, thank you for this time of learning and fellowship. Thank you for the insights you've given us related to your plan for strengthening our families. Help us to set aside time this week to talk about specific ways we can strengthen our families, beginning by completing our homework assignments. Amen.

After Class

Homework
1. Discuss the class session. What new insight(s) or understanding(s) did you gain? What do you believe will be of greatest benefit to you/your family?

_____

_____

2. How much uninterrupted "alone time" or "marriage time" do you spend together on a typical day? Talk about times and ways you can increase and/or protect the amount of time you spend alone together on a daily basis. Beginning this week, try to spend at least 10 minutes of uninterrupted time alone together each day. Here are some things to talk about (each on a separate day):

- Discuss the three primary love languages (p. 38). Write down on a piece of paper what you think your primary love language is, and what you think your partner's love language is. Now share your answers. Discuss ways you can express your love for your spouse using his or her primary love language and record your ideas below.

  _____

  _____

- Review the list of ways to grow spiritually as a couple found on page 00. How many of these things do you currently do? Which of these things would you like to begin doing?

  _____

  _____

- Get out your calendars and schedule several "date nights" for the coming weeks. (Make this a habit at the beginning of each month, or plan several months in advance.) Talk about what you might like to do on these nights and make arrangements for childcare, if necessary. Don't let anything, except for emergencies or unavoidable circumstances, to keep you from breaking these dates! While you have the calendar out, make plans for an overnight or weekend getaway within the next three to six months.

3. As a family—perhaps during mealtime—talk together about the family traditions you currently observe. How many of these traditions have been "passed down"? How many are unique to your family? If you don't have any traditions that are your very own, encourage the children to help you create one. Then, enjoy anticipating and preparing to celebrate your new tradition!

"Passed Down" Traditions	New Traditions
_____	_____
_____	_____
_____	_____

4. If your schedule permits, make plans for a family activity this week; or schedule one for the near future. Begin trying to identify what your "signature" family activity might be.

Tools and Tips

Forming a Family Identity

- Don't try to "force" a family identity by making family members do an activity they don't want to do. Remember, a "signature" family identity has to be fun for everyone. If after several tries the activity is not a "hit," keep trying until you find something everyone will enjoy.
- If your family's "signature" activity is seasonal (such as boating), be sure to have one for the other half of the year (such as ice skating or watching movies together).
- Allow the children to take turns choosing activities the family can enjoy together. Consider having a family night once a week for this purpose.
- Some families make the mistake of trying to cram too many family traditions into one holiday! Select a few meaningful traditions for each holiday and focus on these; otherwise, you run the risk of overwhelming the children and losing the meaning behind the traditions.
- In addition to continuing traditions that have been passed down, create some new family traditions that are unique to your family.
- Find ways to have more fun together!

Rules for Healthy Conflict in Marriage

- Remember that no issue is more important than your relationship. Even when you compromise your personal preferences, you still win because you are safeguarding your marriage.
- Choose a time when you're not having conflict to talk about ways that you each find hurtful and helpful in resolving differences; use this information to guide the way you handle conflicts.
- When conflict occurs, adopt the attitude of "We have a problem" rather than "You are a problem."
- Always attack the problem and not each other.
- Make certain that you understand and respect each other's feel-

ings and opinions about the issue causing the conflict. Then work together to come up with an acceptable way to resolve the problem.

(Adapted from "Keeping Marriage Alive," Robert and Jeanette Lauer, FaithHome for Parents, Abingdon Press, 2001, p.6)

Ways to Tell Your Spouse, "I Love You"

- Express in words how much you love and appreciate your spouse. No one can hear those words too often.
- Write your spouse love notes. Mail them or leave them in unexpected places for your spouse to find.
- Stay physically connected. Hug, kiss, and hold hands whenever you can.
- Plan romantic adventures. These don't have to be expensive. How about a walk in the park, watching a sunset, or taking a bubble bath together.
- Be a friend to your spouse. Be the kind of person your spouse admires, enjoys, and trusts.
- Recall shared experiences you cherish and work together to create more of them.
- Now add your own!

(Adapted from "Keeping Your Marriage Alive," Robert and Jeanette Lauer, FaithHome for Parents, pp. 6-7)